This bright white streak is on the back of a little creature with a loud voice.

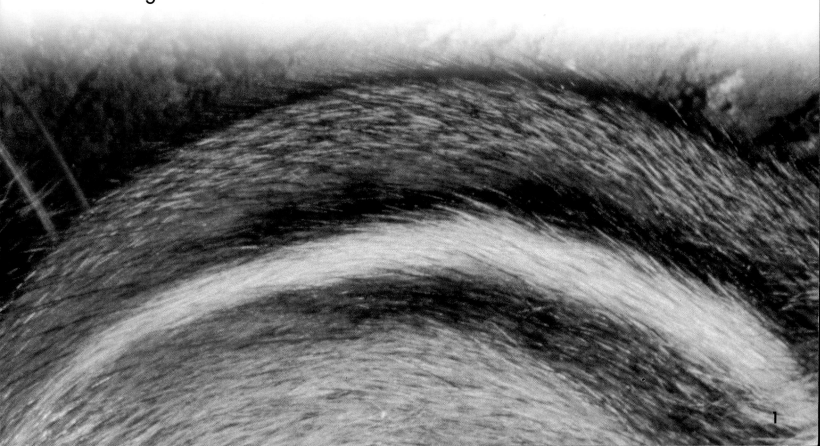

In summer and fall,
chipmunks are busy gathering food.
They carry nuts, seeds,
and fruit in their cheek pouches.
Then they bury the food
in underground dens.

A chipmunk's den
has many little rooms.
Some are for sleeping and
some are for storing food.
When winter comes,
the chipmunk will eat
its hidden food.

If you get too close
to this scaly leg,
it will disappear
inside a shell!

This is a box turtle.
When scared, a box turtle
pulls itself into its shell,
tight as a box.
Some people keep
box turtles as pets.
They can live
40 years or more.

These are not little eggs of a creepy-crawly.
They are from a plant that carpets the forest floor.

Ferns have tiny brown balls underneath their leafy parts.
The balls are called "spore cases." When the cases are ripe,
millions of tiny spores fly away with the wind. Some land nearby
and some travel very far. A few will grow into new ferns.

Is this part of a tree? Is it part of a rock? No, it is from the head of a big, bellowing fellow who lives in the northern woods.

A bull moose wears a crown of antlers.
In the summertime,
these antlers are covered
with soft, furry skin called "velvet."
In the fall, the velvet falls off.
The hard, bony antlers will soon
fall off, too. Next spring,
the bull moose will grow new antlers.
They will be even bigger
than this year's antlers.

This looks feathery, but it is not from a bird.
It belongs to an animal that flutters around at night.

It is one antenna of a big, colorful cecropia moth. The male moth has two feathery antennae. He uses them like a nose. A male moth can smell female moths three miles away!

What is at the other end
of this black-tipped tail?

It is an ermine, or short-tailed weasel. In the summer,
an ermine's fur is dark. By winter, the ermine turns snow white,
except for its black-tipped tail. Why do you think an ermine changes its coat?

What tree has bark
that looks like paper?

A white birch is also called
"paper birch." You can see why!
Years ago, Native Americans
used papery birch bark
to make canoes.

Birch bark has many layers.
The outer layers peel naturally,
but the inner layers make
a tight seal around the tree's trunk.
Never peel a birch's bark
or you might harm its "skin."
If water and insects get in,
they can hurt the tree.

A.

B.

C.

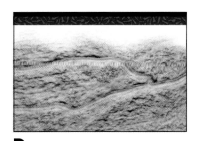
D.

E.

F.

G.

Look closely. Can you name these plants and animals?

A. Chipmunk

B. Box turtle

C. Fern

D. Bull moose

E. Cecropia moth

F. Ermine

G. White birch